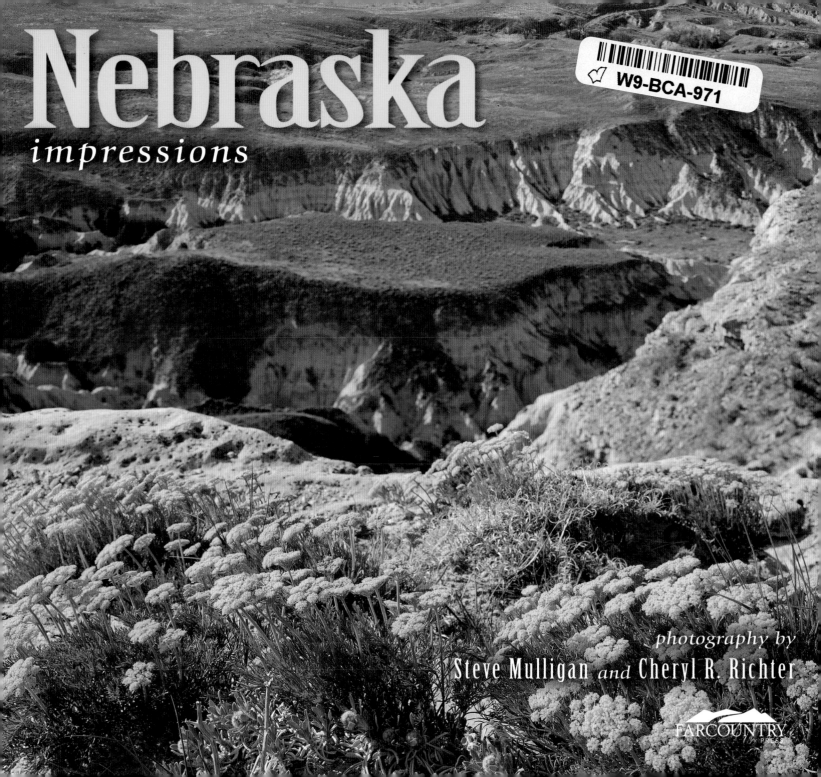

Nebraska
impressions

photography by
Steve Mulligan *and* Cheryl R. Richter

FARCOUNTRY
PRESS

Right: Nebraska is known for images such as this: wind ruffling a wheat field bordered by a windbreak. CHERYL R. RICHTER

Title page: Narrow-leaved musineon blooms on 3,000-acre Scotts Bluff National Monument. The bluff was a prominent natural landmark for emigrants who traveled across the prairie on the Oregon Trail from 1841 to the mid-1860s. STEVE MULLIGAN

Front cover: In early summer, blazing star wildflowers splash the prairie with color in Ponca State Park. STEVE MULLIGAN

Back cover: The tallgrass prairie spreads wide across the landscape near Garland. CHERYL R. RICHTER

ISBN 10: 1-56037-393-8
ISBN 13: 978-1-56037-393-3
Photography © 2006 by Steve Mulligan and Cheryl R. Richter
© 2006 Farcountry Press

For more information about our books write Farcountry Press, P.O. Box 5630, Helena, MT 59604; call (800) 821-3874; or visit www.farcountrypress.com.

Created, produced, and designed in the United States. Printed in China.

10 09 08 07 06   1 2 3 4 5

Above: Delicate purple and white crocuses herald spring on the prairie. CHERYL R. RICHTER

Right: Lush Asiatic lilies thrive in Nebraska's warm, humid summer climate. CHERYL R. RICHTER

Left: These banks of flowers are part of the two-acre display gardens at the Bluebird Nursery in Clarkson. Harlan Hamernick and his wife Shirley began the nursery as a hobby in 1958; today the business ships perennials to garden centers throughout the United States and Canada. CHERYL R. RICHTER

Left: A wintertime view of Willow Island on the 310-mile-long Platte River in Dawson County.   STEVE MULLIGAN

Below: Antarctic penguins mill about a seventy-foot-long acrylic tunnel in Omaha's Henry Doorly Zoo, which evolved from the Riverview Park Zoo established in 1894.   CHERYL R. RICHTER

Right: Arbor Lodge is the stately fifty-two-room neo-colonial mansion completed in 1903 by Joy Morton, the oldest son of J. Sterling Morton, founder of Arbor Day.
CHERYL R. RICHTER

Facing page: Cornfields—such as this one near Macy—are a common sight in the Cornhusker State, which is the nation's third-largest producer of corn. CHERYL R. RICHTER

Left: Sailboats skim the surface of Branched Oak Lake, a 1,780-acre man-made lake that is the largest of ten Salt Creek Flood Control Project dams.
CHERYL R. RICHTER

Far left: Named for the famous Ponca chief, the 3,000-foot Chief Standing Bear Memorial Bridge crosses the Missouri River and connects South Dakota Highway 37 and Nebraska Highways 12 and 14.
CHERYL R. RICHTER

Right: Omaha's thirteen-story Desert Dome in the Henry Doorly Zoo recreates geological features—including a sand dune and mountain—from the Namib Desert of southern Africa, the Red Center of Australia, and the Sonoran Desert of the southwest United States. CHERYL R. RICHTER

Below: The sculpture *Mosaicycle,* by Colleen K. Hake, is part of the Tour de Lincoln, bicycle-themed public art along Lincoln's large network of bicycle trails. CHERYL R. RICHTER

Left: The blossoms of a prairiefire crabapple tree are a stunning deep fuchsia. The tree is a popular landscape planting in Nebraska. CHERYL R. RICHTER

Far left: A springtime profusion of pink flowers adorns a royalty crabapple tree in Lincoln's Woods Park. CHERYL R. RICHTER

Below: Golden Russet apples are one of 160 heirloom varieties grown in the Grosvenor M. Porter Preservation Orchard at Arbor Day Farm in Nebraska City. CHERYL R. RICHTER

Above: Looking like a seven-member bovine board of directors, these Hereford cattle are a common sight in a state that raises nearly 6 million head of cattle. CHERYL R. RICHTER

Right: Near Clarkson, rows of soybeans curve toward the horizon. CHERYL R. RICHTER

Below: A young fancy-dancer performs at the Omaha Tribe of Nebraska's Annual Harvest Celebration and Powwow, held each August in Macy. CHERYL R. RICHTER

Above: Archie Little, a member of the Lakota tribe, wears traditional dress at a festival at Fort Calhoun that celebrates the Corps of Discovery's first council with the Missouri and Oto Indians at Council Bluff in 1804. CHERYL R. RICHTER

Left: Ranch land stretches from horizon to horizon along Nebraska Highway 26 between Ogallala and Lewellen. CHERYL R. RICHTER

Above: Two young dancers take a spin at the Czech Festival in Wilber that features Czech music, dancing, and food. CHERYL R. RICHTER

Facing page: On home football game Saturdays, the downtown streets of Lincoln are ablaze with red as fans show support for The Big Red, or the University of Nebraska Cornhuskers. CHERYL R. RICHTER

Below: A young dancer twirls her skirt at the Cristo Rey Festival, a celebration of the Hispanic community in Lincoln. CHERYL R. RICHTER

Left: Rising above a frothing fountain, the 400-foot Nebraska State Capitol was built from 1922 to 1932 of limestone and features artwork commemorating Nebraska history.
CHERYL R. RICHTER

Far left: This farm scene was created for the sand sculpture competition at the Nebraska State Fair.
CHERYL R. RICHTER

Above: Brilliant goldenrod has been the Nebraska state flower since 1895.
CHERYL R. RICHTER

Right: Eagle Rock is one of several bluffs that make up Scotts Bluff National Monument, an important landmark for the thousands of emigrants who traveled west on the Oregon Trail. STEVE MULLIGAN

Left: These deer are just a few of the 500 mounts—including bighorn sheep, polar bears, and mountain lions—featured in the showroom of Cabela's in Sidney. Dick Cabela started the company in 1961, and it has grown into the nation's largest mail order, retail, and internet outdoor outfitter.
CHERYL R. RICHTER

Far left: A rainbow colors the sky above Fort Robinson State Park in Chadron County.   STEVE MULLIGAN

Below: This skeleton of a wooly mammoth is displayed in Morrill Hall at the University of Nebraska State Museum. The museum's natural history exhibits include a premier collection of fossil elephants, many of which were found on the Great Plains.
CHERYL R. RICHTER

Left: Tallgrass prairie blows gently across the Bohemian Alps, a range of uplands about sixty miles west of and roughly parallel to the Missouri River that was settled by Czech immigrants. The area is celebrated in *Local Wonders: Seasons in the Bohemian Alps* by U.S. poet laureate Ted Kooser. CHERYL R. RICHTER

Below: White pelicans wade in the waters of the Platte River, searching for fish. CHERYL R. RICHTER

Right: Frost outlines the branches of sumac trees lining the banks of the Snake River at Snake Falls in Cherry County. STEVE MULLIGAN

Far right: Snow-flocked trees stand in rich contrast to a deep-blue sky over Pioneer Park and Nature Center, a 900-acre area in southwestern Lincoln that features wildlife and hiking trails. CHERYL R. RICHTER

Left: Two draft horses wait to perform at the annual Camp Creek Machinery and Threshing Show that has celebrated historic farming methods since 1976.
CHERYL R. RICHTER

Facing page: Sun sets on a grassy swale near Rock Creek Station Historical Park.
STEVE MULLIGAN

Below: Re-enactors cross Nebraska on their way to Utah in celebration of the settlers who traveled the Mormon Trail.
CHERYL R. RICHTER

Above: Maple leaf rag: brilliant leaves float in a pool on the Elkhorn River. STEVE MULLIGAN

Left: Autumn paints the trees along the Platte River bluffs in Eugene T. Mahoney State Park near Ashland in hues of orange, red, and green. The park features a lodge and cabins and offers golfing, hiking, and swimming. STEVE MULLIGAN

Right: At Arbor Lodge in Nebraska City, more than 300 participants in the Nebraska Volunteer Infantry re-enact the Civil War Battle of Chalk Bluff using twelve cannons and a Gatling gun. CHERYL R. RICHTER

Below: The 308-foot Great Platte River Road Archway Monument that spans the interstate near Kearney celebrates the evolution of this road, from the wagon train route of emigrants in the 1850s to the nation's first interstate, Interstate 80. CHERYL R. RICHTER

Left: Rabbitbrush blooms in a crevice of the erosion-sculpted rock in Toadstool Geologic Park in the Oglala National Grassland near Crawford. The area is known as the badlands at Nebraska. Located on the Pine Ridge Escarpment near Crawford, the sediments in these landscapes contain immensely valuable fossil deposits.
STEVE MULLIGAN

Far left: Wild indigo, a member of the pea family, greets spring in the Toadstool Badlands.
STEVE MULLIGAN

Right: Sandhill cranes existed in Nebraska more than 9 million years ago, long before there was a Platte River. The river, by comparison, is only 10,000 years old.
CHERYL R. RICHTER

Far right: The 680-mile North Platte River, a tributary of the Platte River, flows through Morrill County on its journey through Nebraska, Colorado, and Wyoming.
STEVE MULLIGAN

Left: Located in the Homestead National Monument, forty miles south of Lincoln near Beatrice, the Palmer-Epard cabin is representative of the homestead cabins built in the late 1800s. CHERYL R. RICHTER

Far left: The landforms in the Pine Ridge Butte National Recreation Area were sculpted over time by wind and water. CHERYL R. RICHTER

Below: Located in Ash Hollow State Historical Park, this stone marker identifies the path of the Oregon Trail. The deep, four-mile-long hollow was a favorite stopover for the emigrants headed west. CHERYL R. RICHTER

Right: Pelican Lake, located in the Valentine National Wildlife Refuge, is popular with fishermen who are attracted by the wide variety of fish, including black bull-head, bluegill, large mouth bass, and perch. The refuge was established in 1935 to protect the Sand Hills region and its wildlife.
STEVE MULLIGAN

Far right: The North Platte River, in Morrill County, flows west to its confluence with the South Platte River in western Nebraska.
STEVE MULLIGAN

Left: The confluence of two grand rivers—the Niobrara and the Missouri—happens at Niobrara State Park. STEVE MULLIGAN

Below: The 230-acre Nine-Mile Prairie is a tallgrass prairie so named because it is five miles west and four miles north of the University of Nebraska campus in downtown Lincoln. CHERYL R. RICHTER

The 19,131-acre Fort Niobrara National Wildlife Refuge along the Niobrara River features plants and wildlife representative of the northern Great Plains and of areas to the east, west, north, and south. STEVE MULLIGAN

Left: The long-legged burrowing owl, with its distinctive *quick-quick-quick,* is the smallest of owls—it stands only nine inches tall. CHERYL R. RICHTER

Facing page: The clay and sandstone Courthouse Rock and the nearby Jail Rock were well-known landmarks along the Oregon Trail. Courthouse Rock towers above the plains, rising to the height of a thirty-two-story building. STEVE MULLIGAN

Below: The greater prairie chicken, with its distinctive markings, was once a common species on the prairies, but as the number of grasslands has declined, so has the number of prairie chickens. CHERYL R. RICHTER

Left: These loess cliffs rise above the Republican River in Webster County of southern Nebraska. Loess is windblown soil often found in this area in cliffs or road cuts and it is excellent for farming. STEVE MULLIGAN

Below: Located at Fort Niobrara National Wildlife Refuge, thundering Fort Falls is formed when the Niobrara River tumbles over the bedrock. STEVE MULLIGAN

Above: This young girl hugs her tree seedling, a gift to the children attending the annual Arbor Day celebration at Arbor Lodge in Nebraska City. CHERYL R. RICHTER

Facing page: A Norway spruce lends cool shade to the seventy-two-acre grounds of Arbor Lodge State Historical Park, one of 270 varieties of trees and shrubs. STEVE MULLIGAN

Below: The creamy white of a mayapple blossom is set off by a bed of green ferns. STEVE MULLIGAN

Left: The tall stalks of a narrow-leafed yucca stand surrounded by the tallgrass prairie. STEVE MULLIGAN

Below: In Antelope County, fuzzy-headed dandelions bloom in profusion beneath a stand of cottonwoods, the species that serves as Nebraska's state tree. STEVE MULLIGAN

Right: A bison stands on the prairie at Fort Robinson State Park, west of Crawford. The home of a post-Civil War military fort that was active until World War II, the area also features such wildlife as turkeys, deer, bison, and antelope.   STEVE MULLIGAN

Below: Dimpled and undulating sand dunes and soil characterize the unique Sand Hills region.   STEVE MULLIGAN

Right: Smith Falls, which begins as a spring-fed creek, tumbles seventy feet to the Niobrara Valley below and is Nebraska's highest waterfall.
STEVE MULLIGAN

Facing page: Driftwood lines the shores of the Platte River as it flows through the Sjogren Wilderness Tract. STEVE MULLIGAN

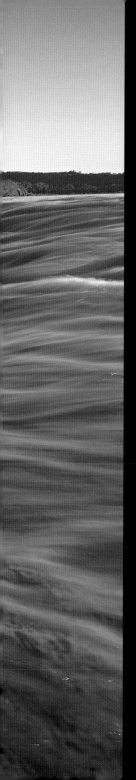

Left: Norden Drop is an example of some of the rapids, riffles, and more than 200 waterfalls along the seventy-six-mile length of the Wild and Scenic Niobrara River. STEVE MULLIGAN

Below: A cloud of cottonwood seeds floats under the trees at the Rock Creek Station Recreation Area, part of a 390-acre state recreation area and historical park established in 1980. STEVE MULLIGAN

Above: Held each summer in the rodeo town of Burwell, the Old-Timers Rodeo features six rodeo events, but participants must be over forty years of age. CHERYL R. RICHTER

Facing page: A covered wagon stands in mute testimony to the thousands of emigrants who stopped at Rock Creek to resupply their wagons and to camp. STEVE MULLIGAN

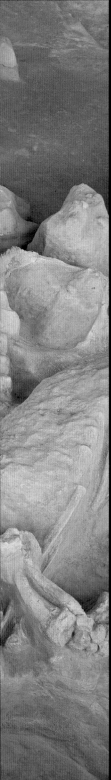

Left: On the banks
of the Missouri River,
Indian Cave features
petroglyphs, the only
known example of
their kind found
in the state.
STEVE MULLIGAN

Far left: These rhino
fossils are just one of
the seventeen species
of vertebrates recov-
ered in the Ashfall
Fossil Beds, now a
state historical park.
STEVE MULLIGAN

Right: This statue of J. Sterling Morton, pioneer Nebraska journalist and horticultural-ist, stands on the grounds of Arbor Lodge.   CHERYL R. RICHTER

Far right: Burchard Lake, the 150-acre lake created in 1951, is a popular spot with birders, who come in spring to hear the prairie chickens booming.
STEVE MULLIGAN

Right: Evening sunset reddens the skies and the waters of manmade Holmes Lake in Lincoln.   CHERYL R. RICHTER

Below: Chimney Rock rises nearly 300 feet above the surrounding North Platte River Valley. It served as a landmark along the Oregon Trail, California Trail, and Mormon Trail, which passed by the north side of the rock.   STEVE MULLIGAN

Left: Stately cottonwoods shade this creek bed in Chadron State Park. STEVE MULLIGAN

Below: The large cave of the 2,386-acre Indian Cave State Park was created when silt and fine-grained sand were deposited in a Pennsylvanian rock channel. STEVE MULLIGAN

Above: Towering above North Platte is this image of Buffalo Bill, who organized the world-famous *Buffalo Bill's Wild West Show* on a ranch near North Platte in 1883. STEVE MULLIGAN

Facing page: Standing tall against the broad, cloud-flecked sky, Courthouse Rock remains a beacon for travelers today. STEVE MULLIGAN

Below: Carhenge, the automobile-age version of the famous Stonehenge, is a popular tourist attraction in Alliance, Nebraska. STEVE MULLIGAN

Right: Delicately shaped and flaming red, columbine lines the banks of Rock Creek in Jefferson County. STEVE MULLIGAN

Below: The quiet waters of Stone Creek flow over a ledge in the deep woodlands of 418-acre Platte River State Park near Louisville. STEVE MULLIGAN

A lightning strike during a violent prairie thunderstorm parallels Scotts Bluff National Monument.
STEVE MULLIGAN

Steve Mulligan

Landscape-photographer Steve Mulligan runs a stock photography business from his home in Moab, Utah. He travels extensively, spending a great deal of time photographing the Nebraska landscape with his large-format 4x5 camera. *Outdoor Photographer* magazine named Steve a Master Landscape Photographer in 1999. His work was featured in the Kodak Professional Photographers' Showcase at Epcot Center, and his recent black-and-white book *EarthWorks* was chosen as photography book of the year by *Black and White Photographer* magazine.

Pictured are Steve and his daughter Alyssa.
www.mulliganphotography.com

Cheryl R. Richter

Born and raised in Nebraska, Cheryl understands the subtle nature of the Cornhusker State and its residents. Her degree from the University of Nebraska Lincoln College of Business Administration and a first career as a certified public accountant taught her the discipline and attention to detail necessary for the technical aspects of photography.

Her images have been published in a diverse group of books, magazines, calendars, cards, and catalogs. Magazine credits include *AAA Living, American Forests, Audubon, Better Homes & Gardens Special Interest Publications, Fine Gardening, Midwest Living, Montana,* and Reiman Publications. Book credits include *The Nebraska Adventure, Making the Most of Shade, America the Beautiful, Shakespeare's Flowers, Sunset's Midwest Top 10 Gardening Guide, In Praise of Apples, From Clay to Bricks,* and Time-Life, Ortho, and Farcountry Press books. Brown & Bigelow, Teldon, Terrell, and Smith Southwestern have used Cheryl's images in their calendars and cards.

Cheryl is a charter member of the North American Nature Photography Association and the Garden Writer's Association of America. Her award-winning images have been recognized by *Outdoor & Travel Photography, Photographer's Forum Magazine,* and *Nature's Best Photography Magazine.*

www.agpix.com/cherylrichter